POPPY SEEDS

Wick Poetry Chapbook Series Five
Catherine Wing, Editor

Poppy Seeds   Allison Davis
Here Both Sweeter   Daniel Carter

POPPY SEEDS

Poems by Allison Davis

The Kent State University Press
Kent, Ohio

Ohio Arts Council
A STATE AGENCY
THAT SUPPORTS PUBLIC
PROGRAMS IN THE ARTS

The Wick Poetry Series is sponsored in part by the Wick Poetry Center at Kent State
University.

Cataloging information for this title is available at the Library of Congress.

17 16 15 14 13   5 4 3 2 1

To my mother, my father, Marla, Suzanne, and Laura

CONTENTS

ACKNOWLEDGMENTS

Thank you to the editors of *Prick of the Spindle* where "Summer Contours" first appeared. I am grateful for The George and Emily Severinghaus Beck Fund Scholarship for Study at Vilnius Yiddish Institute during which many of these poems were written.

For their encouragement and guidance, I'd like to thank Angela Pitinii, Kathy Fagan, Henri Cole, Andrew Hudgins, Joanie Mackowski, Tom LeClair, David Miller, Neil Jacobs, Jack Hay, and Vivian Axiotis McGarrity. My gratitude to my family extends back many generations.

POPPY SEEDS

Dominikonų Gatvė

Mother, his teeth were full of poppy seeds,
his teeth exact as the cobblestones.
The cobblestones covered in pigeons,

Mother, and the white paper bag from the bakery
rattles with leftover poppy seeds
with noise so violet, so sharp

that all of my vowels become poppy seeds,
Mother, his name was all vowels like poppy seeds
dotted over the yellow sun.

I crossed an ocean. It crossed me.
His eyes I exchanged for poppy seeds,
Mother, for afternoon sun from the trolley cars,

for standing in line at the bakery,
pointing to sweet rolls with poppy seeds
while cathedrals rush from the alleyways,

Mother, while love rushes away like a spire.

TO DEVORAH MAZUR

Dumbrova Bialystocka, Poland—Montréal, Canada

> "I have married and married the speech of strangers."
> —Charles Reznikoff

Another language formed your lips. How true
your forest of oaks between which I fit
my fits. It's a species of longing
harshly for a tongue burnt by a bit
of sun. Watered down by an Atlantic,
the word for *here,* for *now,* and
hip bones shattered (no language calms this)
into leaves, a bitter trickle
of a tree, a root word dripping
down to this like a broken faucet
and this, a blind frustration, a fist, my fist
knows your mouth like a wrecking ball.
Seamstress, I've lost the way to unstitch
your tongue from its root-bound mouth.

OCCUPATION

The tailor looks at the page
like he looks at the eye of his needle.

The tailor unstitches the alphabet
so he can reuse the lines.

When the world unravels,
the tailor runs it between his lips.

When the tailor is out of thread,
he invents separation.

When the tailor ties a knot,
he's telling the truth.

DISTANCES

The shape of morning shifts
between my body

and your body, shifts
and closes off

as a nipple skirts
a shoulder.

The shape between the church bell
and the clapper

allows the ringing. It rings
the ache of distance

closing. But the church bells
are not for us. The summer wind

striking against the branches
is not for us.

My mother is for us,
but for how long.

The shape of morning opens
as we talk into the future

on a ladder stretched over
nothing. You talk deep into

the calendar,
enough to last for months.

It's not until we've parted
for seasons

that we'll finally run into
the ending,

a sudden space: a silence
between two strangers on a bus—

a bell between them muted,
swallowing its sound.

LANGUAGE LESSON

"Do you remember *the body*?"
And how. I remember your arm across me
like a weather vane
pointing east, the conjugations of ankle
around a shoulder. I remember driving you to the edge
of your body like the edge of the town
and there, I had you alone. How you held,
how your memory keeps and keeps,
your eyes closed like a store
on the Sabbath, on the Sabbath
I remembered restraint, dividing my body
from your attention feral as wildflowers.
Yes, I remember your body.
As you sped toward me
I crossed myself like a train.

TIMING

You are handsome as high noon,
as all the famous clocks

striking high noon. When I asked
the length

of love, you split
my lips in seconds,

you broke the hands
off the clock.

I put them in a vase.
The leftover ticking

crowded,
bent-fender

furious, its overlap blunting
against our ears.

Your hands broke off
my hips

as I finally half
passed you, as I kissed

clock after clock until
pulse plus pulse

lurched forward,
until all down the hallway

night reordered itself
into a dawn.

ON A THEME BY MOYSHE KULBAK

"די דרייצנטע ווייב האָט געשמט פֿאַר אַ וועדמע אין ליטע"
"His thirteenth wife, who passed for a witch in Lithuania."
—Moyshe Kulbak, trans. from the Yiddish by Leonard Wolf

His fourth finger, with wedding rings stacked to the knuckle.
His father's name, which passed for horseshit in Warsaw.
His dry spell, when he daily flicked off the river.
His first sin, which even god was impressed with.
His tenth boss, who fired and fired him nightly.
His eighteenth winter, when he looked in the eyes of his sweetheart.
His nineteenth winter, when he kicked snow in the eyes of his sweetheart.
His twentieth winter, when he broke branches and made himself antlers.
His fourth bar, where he got drunk and took match to his papers.
His third fear: he'd get drunk, forget his name, and not have his papers.
His old street, where he pounded on every door frame.
His last bet, where he knocked then slumped down the door frame.
The moon—which he hated for many good reasons—
the moon, which he turned from and took twenty paces.
His shadow that he spit on till it shined.

GUST MARTIN

Sea

His teeth were continental, darkly
split by ocean. On his merchant marine
ID, his lips are closed. His English, broken,
breaking against the margins of the sea.

His mouth—dormant with unused muscles—grew
fluent in tongues of water. The waves
broke open, erupting in all
their language, sometimes swearing in Dutch,
sweet-talking in German. Sometimes they still spoke Greek
and he remembered when water was water.

The crew sang *Heave ho! My lads,*
heave ho! Damn the submarine!
until the sea rotted the bows
of their lips. The doctors restitched each
like binding an atlas.

Back home, he swayed like a sailor—the traffic lights,
held at a distance in his eyes,
buoyed beneath their wires
above the snowy Pennsylvania streets.

What can a man do
once he talks his way back
to a wilderness? He grew strange to himself
at kitchen tables. One morning
he heard his wife whisper
his bastard English
into a pot of boiling water. He watched her drift away
while she spoke starboard to the spices.

THE MERCHANT MARINE'S WIFE

New Castle, Pennsylvania

You wake up before the children and boarders
and stand in the kitchen doorway in your nightgown.
Beams of sunlight crack at the counters
and break across the floor. Your blood
goes blackstrap, circles gleam yellow-violet

beneath your eyes. At the counter you curve
a paring knife around an orange, your thumb flared
against the blade, the fruit's weight rolling
seasick in your palm. Bitter citrus and the linoleum walk
of your feet. You lift the window. Hydrangeas crowd against
the screen of aluminum mesh. Blackbirds snap like oil
hitting a pan: a heated argument
you heard once then forgot, a young bride

moving across the empty architecture
of an ocean. Where others had pulse
you had rough twigs
to protect your silence. No one knows this,
and for that, you've been lucky.
Your husband comes and goes
across the waters, his blood

turned tide. What a match, you two,
to start a stove with. What a quiet morning,
an orange the only witness to the language
you share with flowers. Immaculate atlas,
how did you get here—so far from everything—
for a man who picks at your bones
while your breasts swell up with sea?

SUMMER CONTOURS

Grass: a wet ink alphabet
crystallized under nectar. Perimeters crack with apricots
& figs. Birds rustle thick in almond
branches, chirping roughly

at eye-level. A man reads
the paper on the patio. He goes to close the windows
but stops. His wife
hangs laundry, clothespins tight between her
teeth, her grandmother's tablecloth
flung across the line.

Waving, she gathers it
warm around her shoulders.
His eyes sink to her feet, reading subtitles
below her in the grass.

The newsprint scrapes up his yellow blood.

Last night, he looked down the line
of backyards as the moon
must: tree-lined rectangles
of wet grass. The leaves, razor sharp
in the morning, broadened
like pupils in the dark.
This was fine. It was the crickets,
so insistent, the night crowded
with their chirping: *come to me, stay,*
fuck me, darling, fuck off.

His hand drops from the window.
Wind knocks branches against
the screens, shadows shake
like insects over the headlines.
He closes his eyes & sees
flowers bigger than ostrich eggs,

moon-bright. He looks at her ankles, his neckties
hanging still, blacker than a killer's shoes
& more harmonic.

STILL

My body is very dumb.
It still expects you every time

it's horizontal. At the dentist's
it opened its mouth

for you and instead
got jabbed by a circle

that mirrored its pain.
I laughed. I tell my body

how dumb it looks
beneath the muscle

of your memory. I say
enough's enough,

it's been too long, longer
than the rain, its math—

an endless addition
ending in *flood:* a word

that breaks, that washes
away. You went away,

but my body went farther:
dumb thing can't measure.

It waits for the air above
to grow empty and still.

MATRIARCH TO PATRIARCH

I made you swallow a map.
I used up all of your ribs.
You became so handsome
I filled a rolodex
with species of need.

Still you walked to me barefoot in the sand
with the radio static, with the crackle of red
leaves in the campfire, with your mouth
cut roughly with salt and your morning hair
holy with the outskirts of some psalm.

I blame my mind on water mixed with iron.
I knife countries in the blanks between your fingers.
Alphabetically, your elbows fall between
doorknob and *Fourth International.*

And yes, your brothers hate me—
and they have reasons, many good ones—
but none that you could carry,
no, none that would catch your eye.

SPARE REGRETS

Of the proportions etched lipsure
into the ache,

I say: my beauty totals
the eyes that truly

bent into mine, harboring
spring flowers

in lush stabs
all house side, evening-full.

Evening-full,
am I of you,

am I daughter of
if I close your mouth what's left? because

what's left is what
I want, a slant, seasonal,

of mouth on my first-time
mouth until the lip of

you oh all who I frowned beside thinking
this is what will

hurt in the morning:
that I wanted harder, and didn't.

BEAUTIFUL, THE DEAD END

    of your body
strong with the last shards
of summer, beautiful,

Ohio, your children
pushing each other
midwest of decency

toward failure, certain, their nerves
disciples of the end
of August, the season brutal

to the brink of its body,
the mud marked by heels
in sudden monuments

where they forced tameness
back into their eyes, reeling
themselves down

until, half-mass sober,
enough language returned
to think so long, lover

I'll long for as long as
Ohio rivers, beautiful,
letting me go

too far, through orchard
and field, through the best
of the body, beyond

the shards of vows
we leave in each other.
Beautiful, all that leaving.

SYMBIOTIC ECONOMICS

Montréal, Canada

To buy cherries that weighed
and cost less, my great-grandmother
removed their stems, plucking them off
with a concerted look
like she was defeathering hens.

Dragging behind her like a wedding train,
boys with cracked-straw brooms
swept up and down the market floor.

And what the hell do you mean says your father. With all the blank-
    ness in the world
chirps your mother. With all the clocks aiming north
says a cousin. You'll break the bones of the page
says another. You've got us all wrong sing the dead. With lilacs tall
on the bed stand. With wartime
seriousness. With peddlers shouting *kalimera,*
kalimera! outside the window.

KATEDROS AIKŠTĖ / CATHEDRAL SQUARE

A trinket—the sun, and a pigeon—
for the eye. *How goes it by*
you, the summer? August: when the one you left
will find another. All history tied
to the feet of the pigeons;
the church bells strike through
until Sunday's a relic—
a museum full of Sundays
and women complaining
beautifully, in their best clothes.

NOTE

In "Gust Martin," the lines "Heave ho! My lads, heave ho! Damn the submarine!" are from "Heave Ho" (1943), the service song of The U.S. Merchant Marine written by Lt. j.g. Jack Lawrence.